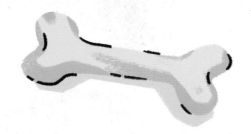

Making Sense of Dog Senses

HOW OUR FURRY FRIENDS EXPERIENCE THE WORLD

WRITTEN BY
Stephanie Gibeault

ILLUSTRATED BY
Raz Latif

Owlkids Books

For Aunt Beth who said, "I always thought you should be a writer." —S.G.

To Harvey and Connor —R.L.

ACKNOWLEDGEMENTS: I would like to express my heartfelt thanks to editor Stacey Roderick, designer Alisa Baldwin, and the rest of the Owlkids team for working with me to develop such a fabulous book. And much gratitude to Jennifer Stokes and Karen Boersma for the opportunity to work with Owlkids Books. My sincere appreciation to Raz Latif for creating the adorable illustrations that not only delight but inform. Additional thanks to my agent Jacqui Lipton, who believed in this from the very start, and to my critique partners for their invaluable feedback and support. Finally, thank you to my mom, Janet, and the rest of my family for always cheering me on.

Text © 2024 Stephanie Gibeault | Illustrations © 2024 Raz Latif

Owlkids Books acknowledges the financial support of the Canada Council for the Arts, the Ontario Arts Council, the Government of Canada through the Canada Book Fund (CBF) and the Government of Ontario through the Ontario Creates Book Initiative for our publishing activities.

Owlkids Books gratefully acknowledges that our office in Toronto is located on the traditional territory of many nations, including the Mississaugas of the Credit, the Chippewa, the Wendat, the Anishinaabeg, and the Haudenosaunee Peoples.

Published in Canada by Owlkids Books Inc., 1 Eglinton Avenue East, Toronto, ON M4P 3A1
Published in the US by Owlkids Books Inc., 1700 Fourth Street, Berkeley, CA 94710

Library of Congress Control Number: 2023939180

Library and Archives Canada Cataloguing in Publication

Title: Making sense of dog senses : how our furry friends experience the world / written by Stephanie Gibeault ; illustrated by Raz Latif.
Names: Gibeault, Stephanie, author. | Latif, Raz, illustrator.
Description: Includes bibliographical references and index.
Identifiers: Canadiana (print) 20230467970 | Canadiana (ebook) 20230468020 | ISBN 9781771475242 (hardcover) | ISBN 9781771476089 (EPUB)
Subjects: LCSH: Dogs—Sense organs—Juvenile literature. | LCSH: Dogs—Physiology—Juvenile literature. | LCSH: Dogs—Behavior—Juvenile literature. | LCSH: Senses and sensation—Juvenile literature.
Classification: LCC SF768.2.D6 G53 2024 | DDC j636.7/08928—dc23

Edited by Stacey Roderick | Designed by Alisa Baldwin

MIX
Paper from responsible sources
FSC® C104723

Manufactured in Guangdong Province, Dongguan City, China, September 2023, by Toppan Leefung Packaging & Printing (Dongguan) Co., Ltd. Job #BAYDC128

hc   A   B   C   D   E   F

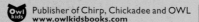
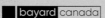
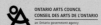

Publisher of Chirp, Chickadee and OWL
www.owlkidsbooks.com

Owlkids Books is a division of bayard canada

ONTARIO ARTS COUNCIL
CONSEIL DES ARTS DE L'ONTARIO
an Ontario government agency
un organisme du gouvernement de l'Ontario

Canada Council for the Arts   Conseil des Arts du Canada

Canada

—Table of Contents—

Making Sense of Dog Senses

Considering humans and dogs have been best friends for thousands of years, we don't have very much in common. Do *you* roll in poop and drink out of the toilet bowl? Ew, no way! So why do dogs? Because these behaviors make sense in a *dog*-sense way.

We humans experience our environment using a combination of our main senses: sight, smell, taste, touch, and hearing. So do many other animals. But every type of animal has a set of senses that is specially adapted to their habitat and behavior. For example, the ears of a tiny mouse are tuned to the high-pitched squeaks of other mice—sounds too high for your ears. And although you can't hear them, the low-pitched rumbles of elephants can be captured by the ears of another elephant over 0.6 mi. (1 km) away.

So how about dogs? A dog's sense of smell is thousands and thousands of times more sensitive than yours. Does that mean they have superpowered sight and hearing, too? How about touch and taste? This book will explore these five senses, as well as extra senses dogs might have that humans don't. *Dog*-gone it, by the time you finish this book, you'll be able to fully appreciate what the world feels like to our canine companions. And you might even understand their love of poop rolling and toilet-water drinking!

EVERY DOG IS UNIQUE

Just like us, every dog is an individual with different sensory abilities. For example, not all dogs have exactly the same hearing. Breeds with upright ears may be able to hear better than breeds with floppy ears. And there is variation between breeds for the other senses, too. Plus, one dog might lose her sight with age while another might be born deaf. So as you read, keep in mind that the *woof*-tastic senses described in this book are generalities.

MORE THAN FIVE SENSES!

This book focuses on the five main senses because they're the most well-known ones, but people and dogs actually have *more* than five. Scientists think there may be over 30 in total. For example, there's proprioception (pro-pree-oh-SEP-shun), which is your sense of where your body is in space. It allows you to do things like touch your elbow with your eyes closed. Some senses are ones you notice, like knowing when you're hungry. Others you don't notice, like your body responding to the level of oxygen in your blood.

There's a **Wolf** in the **Living Room**

When two dogs greet each other, they don't shake paws—they sniff butts! Why do dogs do something so gross? Because take away their squeaky toys and cute sweaters, and dogs are still animals, after all.

Dogs evolved from wolves. These large carnivores, or meat eaters, are found all over North America, Europe, and Asia. They live in family groups known as packs. A pack defends a territory and often hunts together. Wolves are famous for communicating with each other by howling, but they also use chemical scents, like pee left on trees and rocks to mark their territory.

About 40,000 years ago, there were no dogs, but there were wolves and humans. Back then, humans gathered plants and hunted animals for food. But the animals they ate, such as deer or caribou, were the same ones the wolves hunted. You can bet that put people and wolves in direct competition for dinner.

So how did we eventually become best friends *fur*-ever with our bitter rivals? Scientists aren't positive, because there are no records from that long ago. But based on research using fossils and DNA, there are two main possibilities.

The first is that humans captured wild wolf pups to have as pets, raising them and keeping the tamest ones. (A tame animal is a wild animal who has learned to get along with people.) These tamer pets would have produced pups that were a bit friendlier than the wild wolves. Eventually these animals would have become domesticated, meaning they were born comfortable around humans. After enough generations, these pet wolves became the pet dogs we know today.

The second possibility is that wolves tamed themselves. Early humans produced garbage, which was a tempting food source for animals. Some wolves were too afraid to take advantage of the garbage, but less skittish wolves were attracted to an easy meal. Over generations, the braver wolves became friendly toward humans, and these

wolves bred with each other until eventually they became domesticated dogs.

However it happened, we know that all pet dogs have a predator in their past. And those wolf ancestors shaped how dogs experience the world. So even though today's dogs no longer need to stalk deer together in the dim light of dusk to survive, they still communicate with each other using odors. And since the smelliest place on another dog is their behind, it's no wonder dogs love butt sniffing!

TINY TOYS AND COLOSSAL CANINES

If they're all related, why don't all dogs look like wolves ... or like each other? It's because humans got involved. As soon as dogs started living with us, we began to breed them to behave in certain ways by choosing particular males and females to pair up to have puppies. Then, in the 1800s, dog breeding really took off, and people started breeding dogs for their looks. Today there are over 350 different dog breeds, from tiny ones, such as Yorkshire terriers, to giant ones, such as Great Danes.

Do **You See** What **I See?**

Chi Chi the tiny Chihuahua loves to chase rabbits. If he sees one moving, he explodes into action. The chase continues until the rabbit escapes to safety. But sometimes, if a rabbit stays perfectly still, Chi Chi ignores it. It's as if he doesn't even see it. Why does Chi Chi miss something so obvious? Let's see what dogs can see.

Like a human's, a dog's vision is all about light. Here's how a dog's eye translates light into sight.

First, light passes through the cornea, a clear dome that protects the surface of the eye as well as helps to focus the light. Next, the light enters the eye through the pupil, which is surrounded by the iris. (The iris gives eyes their color. Most dogs have brown eyes, but some have blue or green or even two different-colored eyes.) The iris opens or closes around the pupil to control how much light passes through.

The light then travels through the lens, a clear structure that focuses the light onto the retina along the back of the eyeball. The retina is covered in special cells, called photoreceptors, that sense light. When light activates a photoreceptor, it sends a message along the optic nerve (a bundle of nerve fibers) to the brain. That's when the brain forms an image of the object being seen.

Dogs and humans have two basic types of photoreceptors: cones and rods. Cones are the photoreceptors that see color and details. They need a lot of light to work. Rods work

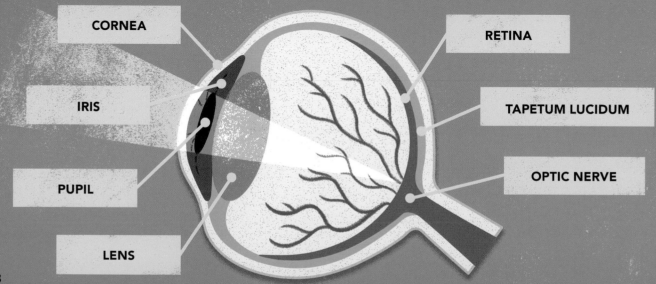

CORNEA

RETINA

IRIS

TAPETUM LUCIDUM

PUPIL

OPTIC NERVE

LENS

in low-light conditions, but they can't detect color. Both humans and dogs have more rods than cones in their eyes, but dogs have far fewer cones overall.

One of the biggest differences between a dog's eye and a human's is that a dog has a triangle of reflective tissue behind the retina. Called the tapetum lucidum (ta-PETE-um LOO-sid-um), it helps dogs see in low light. When light enters the eyeball, some of it is absorbed by the retina. The unabsorbed light passes through the retina, hits the tapetum lucidum, and bounces back to the retina, giving the photoreceptors a second chance to detect the light. If you've ever noticed a dog's eyes glowing at night in the beam of a flashlight, it's because the tapetum lucidum is reflecting the light back at you.

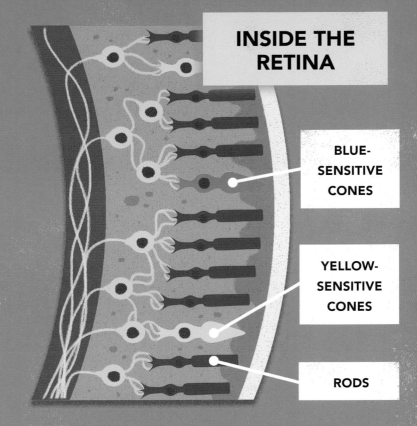

INSIDE THE RETINA

BLUE-SENSITIVE CONES

YELLOW-SENSITIVE CONES

RODS

HIDING IN PLAIN SIGHT

Dogs can see in far lower light than humans because dogs' eyes have so many rods, as well as a tapetum lucidum. But why would that be useful? After all, dogs are mostly awake during the day and asleep at night. Well, remember their wolf ancestors? They hunted in the low light of dawn and dusk because that was the best time for catching prey.

Rods are also great at detecting movement, and because dogs have so many of them, they can probably track moving objects exceptionally well. That's why some dogs can easily pluck a moving tennis ball out of midair. And amazingly, dogs can recognize a faraway object better when it's moving than when it's standing still. That's very handy when your dinner is on the run and you have to catch it. So remember Chi Chi chasing those rabbits? Now you know why he doesn't always notice the ones that stay perfectly still. Smart bunnies!

As **Far** as the Eye Can See

Now let's take a peek at visual acuity. That means how sharp and clear objects look from a distance. Dogs can't tell us what they're seeing so how do we measure that? With stripes!

Scientists created a dog-friendly test using two screens showing black and white stripes. The stripes ran up and down on one screen and side to side on the other. The scientists showed dogs both screens and taught them that they got a treat if they approached a screen with stripes going one way instead of the other. Then it was test time.

Over a series of tests, the scientists made the stripes thinner and thinner until the stripes blurred to gray. When the stripes were really close together, the dogs could no longer tell the screens apart. That showed the limit of their visual acuity.

Then the scientists repeated the experiment with humans and discovered an eye-opening difference! People showed a visual acuity *three times better* than dogs'—this means what most people can see from 60 ft. (18 m) away would need to be within 20 ft. (6 m) for a dog to see it clearly. Of course, making out details in the distance is not as important to dogs. Thanks to their wolf ancestors, dogs have different vision needs, like spotting moving prey.

DOGGY EYEWEAR

If you had the visual acuity of a dog, you would be prescribed glasses. And did you know that there are corrective eyeglasses for dogs, too? Glasses held in place with elastic straps can be worn by dogs with vision loss or cataracts (clouding of the eye's lens). Although visually impaired dogs can rely on their sense of smell to get around (more on that later!), wearing glasses can make a big difference when going up and down the stairs or moving from room to room.

TAKE A LOOK

Follow these steps to compare your visual acuity to a dog's.

1. Type out a short note using a 30-point font size.
2. Print your note and hang it on a wall or even a fridge.
3. See how far away you can stand and still clearly read the words on your note. Mark that spot on the floor.
4. Return to the computer and change the font size in your note to 10.
5. Print this version and hang it on top of your first note.
6. Return to the spot you marked on the floor and see if you can read the second note.

Was the second note blurry? How much closer would you have to stand to read it? This is where a dog would have to stand to see the first note clearly. Now you know how your vision compares to a dog's!

Black and White and Gray All Over?

Have you ever heard that dogs see only in black and white? Well, that's a myth—dogs *paws*-itively can see color! It's just that their world is pretty drab compared to ours.

Why? As you read on page 8, both humans' and dogs' eyes have photoreceptors called cones. Cones are the cells that sense color. But dogs' eyes have only two types of cones, whereas humans' eyes have three. And the cones in a dog's eyes are sensitive to blue and yellow light, while ours are sensitive to red, green, and blue light.

These differences mean that where we see a rainbow of bright colors, dogs see a more limited range of colors, from yellow to blue to gray. To dogs, a red squeaky toy surrounded by green grass is seen entirely in shades of yellow.

But although dogs may not be able to tell yellow, red, and green apart, that's not the whole story. Scientists believe there might be a difference in how dogs perceive the brightness of each color. To a dog, a favorite yellow ball might look like a brighter yellow than a red ball. By using levels of brightness, a dog can still tell which ball is her favorite.

Do you think a dog's blue-and-yellow view of the world means they are missing out? Not at all! Most humans are dependent on their ability to see, but dogs rely more on their supersensitive noses. So does it really matter to a dog if the feast on the dinner table looks like one big gray blob? Unlikely, especially when a dog can catch the scent of every delicious ingredient that went into making dinner.

Follow My Nose

Remi is part Labrador retriever and part magician. No matter where her human hides a five-dollar bill, Remi can find it. Even if there are other distracting smells around, like a hidden piece of hot dog—abracadabra!— she locates the money. What makes Remi's nose so powerful? Let's take a close look at how a dog's nose knows.

When dogs breathe in air through their nostrils, scent particles come along for the ride. Inside the nose, the air separates into two streams. Most of the air travels to the lungs, but some travels to an area at the back of the dog's nose used only for smelling. Once in this area, the air lingers and stays undisturbed when the dog exhales. This gives the dog longer to absorb all the scent particles in that air.

This scent-detecting tissue at the back of a dog's nose is called the olfactory epithelium (ole-FAK-tor-ee eh-puh-THEE-lee-uhm). It contains special cells called olfactory receptors that sense smells. Certain receptors react to certain smells. And each receptor is connected to nerves in the olfactory bulb of the brain.

The olfactory bulb is the part of a dog's brain responsible for filtering and distinguishing between all the different smells. Once the olfactory bulb has sorted the scents, it signals the rest of the brain to react. The brain might decide where the smell is coming from, recall a memory associated with that smell, or respond with an emotion.

A vomeronasal (VOM-ero-NAY-sal) organ sits above the roof of a dog's mouth. Also called the Jacobson's organ, it's a separate scent-detection system that recognizes special chemicals called pheromones (FEHR-uh-mowns). These help dogs communicate with each other. For example, the

DO YOU SMELL THAT?

While a human's sense of smell is nothing to be sniffed at, dogs experience the world through their noses in a way we can only imagine. Not only do they have millions and millions more olfactory receptors than we do, but they also have more kinds of them. Plus, their olfactory epithelium is much, much larger. Finally, a dog's olfactory bulb takes up a far larger portion of their brain than a human's does. All this means that dogs can detect smells too faint for our noses *and* distinguish between them. Now you know the secret to Remi's magic trick!

smell of a mother dog's pheromones will comfort her nursing pups, or a female dog's can indicate her interest in a mate. Dog pee is full of pheromones. So are the anal glands on a dog's rear end, which explains all that butt sniffing.

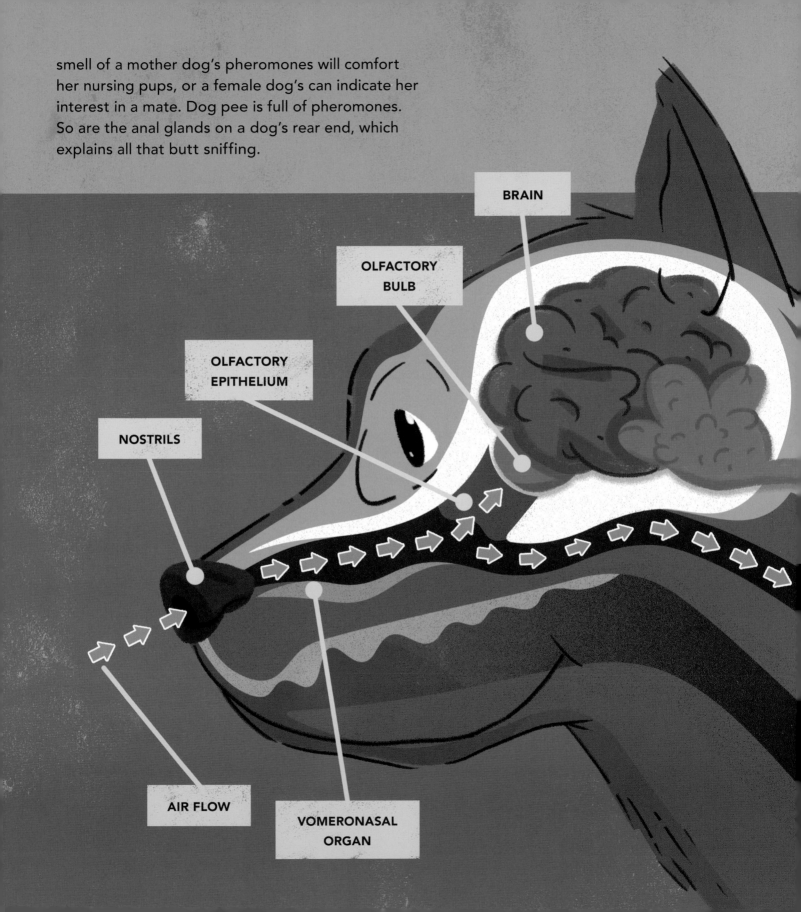

BRAIN

OLFACTORY BULB

OLFACTORY EPITHELIUM

NOSTRILS

AIR FLOW

VOMERONASAL ORGAN

One Big Nose

All dogs are designed for smelling, but bloodhounds are maybe the most famous for their ability to track a scent. Here's a closer look at the parts that make bloodhounds—and other dog breeds—act like one big nose.

NOSE

Why is a dog's nose usually wet? It's to help her smell. The nose is kept moist by a layer of mucus that traps odor particles. This allows the dog to breathe them in on the next inhale.

NOSTRILS

When a dog breathes, air goes in through her nostril holes and out through the slits at the sides. This protects odor molecules already in the dog's nose from being disturbed when air is exhaled. That way, odor molecules are inside the nose for longer and have a better chance of being detected. Breathing out of the nostril slits also helps the dog collect more smells, especially from the ground. How? Air exhaled out of the slits swirls around and kicks up new odor particles. Then on the next inhale, there are more scents for her nostrils to capture. Dogs can even use their nostrils independently: for familiar smells they enjoy, they rely on their right nostril, and for smells they find upsetting, they use their left.

WRINKLES

Breeds such as bloodhounds have so much loose skin, they have deep wrinkles all over their faces. It's thought that these wrinkles also help trap scent particles.

EARS

Long, droopy ear flaps help funnel smells up from the ground toward the dog's nose.

TONGUE

Dogs lick their noses to keep them damp since a dry nose doesn't work as well for collecting scents. Nose licking can also carry odor particles into the mouth and closer to the vomeronasal organ.

FLEWS AND DEWLAPS

Some dog breeds have what look like extra folds of skin on their heads and necks. Long, droopy lips are called flews or jowls. And a flap of sagging skin dangling from a dog's neck is called a dewlap. All this loose skin is not just adorable; it collects and traps smells.

PUPPY POWER

For the first few weeks of a puppy's life, he can't see or hear. But from the moment he's born, he can smell. Thank goodness, because learning his mother's scent is essential for a helpless newborn's survival. He depends on his mother for safety, companionship, and her nutritious milk. Whenever he needs her, he finds her by her scent. In fact, a puppy's sense of smell might even start working in the womb!

17

You Can **Run** but You **Can't Hide**

It makes sense that dogs are born following scents. It's one of the ways their wolf ancestors found prey. And this nosey nature is what allows us to use dogs for tracking. Whether it's a lost child or a criminal on the run, we can give dogs a smell to follow, and off they go. But you might be surprised by all the things a dog can *reek*-ognize when they are on the trail of a scent.

From a dog's perspective, humans stink. We sweat and have oily skin and smelly breath. Many of us use scented laundry soap, lotion, and perfume. And everybody has their own unique odor, even identical twins. On top of that, we shed smelly skin cells wherever we go. Finally, when you walk across the ground, you squish plants, soil, insects, and so on, leaving behind a smell known as a disturbance odor.

But a scent trail could go anywhere—across a field, through woods, or even through a stream. So how do dogs stay on track? They might pay attention to the strength of the smell, since the longer a footprint has been on the ground, the more its scent fades. A dog on a trail will move toward the fresher prints and away from the older ones. In fact, some dogs only need as few as five footsteps to know which prints are freshest and therefore

which direction the person was headed. And this is where dogs' nostrils may be extra useful. When close enough to the smell, dogs get different information in each nostril. By comparing the strength of the smell that goes in the right versus the left nostril, a dog can tell which direction to take.

READING THE DAILY *PEE*-MAIL

Dogs love fire hydrants. They're perfect for bathroom breaks … and for smelling the pee of the dogs who have been there before. Yuck! But don't turn up your nose just yet. Similar to the way dogs' wolf ancestors peed on trees and rocks to communicate with other wolves, dogs can tell a whole lot from these "pee-mail" messages, including another dog's age, health, sex, mood, confidence, and interest in romance. So the local hydrant lets a dog catch up on all the neighborhood gossip with just a sniff.

Sniffing
Superpowers

Although there are other animals with impressive sniffers, such as elephants and mice, they won't walk on a leash or work for kibble. However, dogs are so trainable, we can teach them—in just a few steps—which smells to find. First, they learn to associate a certain smell with a reward, such as a treat or game of tug. Then they must find that smell from a range of samples or out in the real world. When they find it, they get their reward.

There are many jobs in which working dogs are trained to use their superpowered noses.

Some dogs search for explosives. Others are taught to find the poop of endangered species, such as whales. And some even sniff out diseases, such as cancer.

Cancer-detection dogs often make their diagnosis by smelling a person's blood, pee, or breath. Those samples contain thousands of different chemicals, yet a dog can find the smallest trace of unhealthy odor. But dogs don't go to medical school, so how do their noses know?

Dogs can smell just a particle or two of smell in one trillion particles of air. That's like finding a single mint jellybean in a sports stadium filled to the roof with jellybeans! Superpowered noses is right!

TIME-TRAVELING NOSES

A dog's superior sniffer is something of a superpower. For instance, in a way, they can smell the past! How? Because smells fade over time, dogs can sense how long a stink has been lingering around. Dogs can kind of smell the future, too. That's because someone's smell reaches a dog's nose before the person comes through a door or around a corner. Finally, a dog's home and yard smell different in the morning than in the afternoon or evening, and that rhythm of daily scents helps a dog smell the time with her nose.

THE DISAPPEARING SMELL

Believe it or not, humans can detect certain smells, like bananas, even better than dogs. But for many other smells, dogs have the upper paw. Here's a way to test the power of your nose:

1. Put 15 ml (1 tbsp.) of water in a large mixing bowl. Add a drop or two of scent like vanilla or peppermint extract.
2. Stir them together and then smell the mixture.
3. Add 120 ml (½ cup) of water to the mixture and smell it again.
4. Keep adding water 120 ml (½ cup) at a time, smelling your mixture each time. When you can't smell the scent anymore, you've reached your nose's limit.

How much water did you add before the scent disappeared? Could a dog beat you? Probably. Remember that dogs can smell just a few drops of a scent in a swimming pool of water! But try a different scent and see if you can do better.

Pass the Poop

Pepper the French bulldog loves to snuggle, but she also loves to eat. And she'll eat anything. Her owner has even found stuffing from squeaky toys in Pepper's poop, and you know what that means. And once, Pepper ate a dirty diaper! There's no accounting for taste, but surely she can tell the difference between toys, treats, and garbage.

The ability to taste is thanks to tiny sensory organs called taste buds. In humans, these are found in our mouths, mostly clustered together in small bumps called papillae (puh-PIH-lee) all over the surface of our tongues. Individual taste buds contain special receptor cells that sense chemicals in food and then send a message to the brain, which responds to the taste.

A dog's taste buds are mostly found clustered in papillae on his tongue, too, but some are also on the roof of his mouth and at the top of his throat. That way, even when a dog gulps down his dinner or swallows a treat without chewing, he can probably still taste it on its way down.

The more taste buds an animal has, the more sensitive their sense of taste. Dogs have around 1,700 taste buds. That's a lot, but the average human has between 5,000 and 8,000! That means your sense of taste is far better than any dog's. For example, you can taste the subtle differences between flavors of fruit where a dog might just taste sweet. That could help explain why Pepper ate that diaper. She doesn't have bad taste—she simply can't tell when something tastes bad. Or at least what would taste bad to us.

GEE, THAT DIAPER SMELLS DELICIOUS

It's not just a lack of taste buds that explains dogs' questionable eating habits. What we experience as flavor includes more than taste. It also involves other sensations such as a food's texture, temperature, and, most important, smell. A dog might eat something we think is gross because he thinks it smells delicious. How does that work? Early dogs likely survived as scavengers that ate waste left behind by humans, so eating garbage and, yes, poop comes naturally to them.

Fido Has a Meat Tooth

Your taste buds recognize five basic tastes. Sweet is found in sugary foods, such as honey or fruit. Salt is found in your saltshaker or in snacks like salted pretzels. You can taste sour when you eat lemons or plain yogurt. And bitter is found in dark chocolate or brussels sprouts. The fifth taste is a more recent discovery known as umami (oo-MAA-mee). Also called savory, umami is found in foods like meat, mushrooms, or miso. Dogs can recognize these same five tastes, too.

Most dogs get very excited when you offer them a tidbit of steak—thanks to their wolf ancestors, it's no surprise they like meaty tastes. But dogs also have other taste preferences.

Some will do anything for a bit of fruit or veggie. That's because dogs actually have lots of taste receptors for sweetness. But why would a meat eater need to be able to taste sugar? It may be because early dogs ate fruit and other plant parts when meat was hard to find. Having sweetness receptors would have helped them tell when fruit was ripe and ready to eat.

Dogs aren't all that sensitive to the taste of salt, though. And they don't crave it the way humans do. This is probably because meat is a naturally salty food, and so early dogs got more than enough salt in their diet of prey. They didn't need their tongues' salt receptors to help them find more.

24

Finally, many dogs dislike sour foods and detest bitter ones. That's because these tastes may signal that a food is unripe, rotten, or even toxic. So these taste receptors help dogs avoid eating food that might make them sick. And these receptors serve the same purpose for you as well. That's why bitter foods, like brussels sprouts, are an acquired taste for most.

TAKING A BITE OUT OF THE TASTE BUD MYTH

Did you know dogs might have taste receptors for water on the tip of their tongues? (More on that to come!) And maybe you've heard certain parts of your tongue only taste certain things? Like the front of your tongue only tastes sweetness. Well, guess what? Although the edges and tip of your tongue are more sensitive than the middle, your entire tongue can experience all the different tastes. Lick a slice of lemon or a salty potato chip using different parts of your tongue and taste for yourself. *Bone* appétit!

On the **Tip** of the **Tongue**

Dogs may be able to sense a sixth taste—water! Scientists believe the tip of a dog's tongue likely has receptors just for that taste. And after a dog eats sugary or salty foods, these receptors seem to become even more sensitive. This encourages the dog to drink when she needs it most.

Why would these taste buds be located only on the tip of a dog's tongue? Because of how she drinks—and that's more complicated than you might think!

Dogs don't have cheeks like you do, so they can't suck water into their mouths. It would simply fall out the sides if they tried. Instead, it's all about their tongues. A dog curls the tip of her tongue backward and then dunks it into the water. You might guess she's using her tongue like a ladle to scoop water into her mouth. She's not! She's using her tongue to smack the water and create a column of water that rises up and out of the bowl. Then with careful timing, she bites that splash to get a gulp of water. Because the tip of her tongue is the first part to touch the water, it's the part that needs those water-tasting taste buds.

If you want to try drinking water like a dog, be ready with a towel because you're going to make a mess. Fill a bowl with clean water and smack the surface with the top part of your tongue. Then chomp to capture the splash you make. And no curling your tongue like a ladle, because that would be cheating!

SALT SENSITIVITY

Dogs have about a quarter of the taste buds you have. And the ones they have aren't as sensitive to salt. Follow these steps to see how your salt receptors stack up against a dog's.

1. Fill a small bowl with 2 cups (500 ml) of water.
2. Add 1/4 tsp. (1.5 ml) of salt and then stir until it dissolves.
3. Dip your tongue into the water to taste the salt.
4. Add 3/4 tsp. (4.5 ml) more salt to the water and then stir until it dissolves.
5. Dip your tongue again to taste how much saltier the water has become.

You could probably taste the salt the first time, but the second time was super salty, right? A dog might need that much salt in the water to even notice it's there.

Heat-Seeking Noses

Rufus the Bolognese has recently become blind. He uses his memory and the feel of the floor—carpet in the dining room and hardwood in the TV room—to find his way around the house. And when he looks for his owner, he relies on his nose, but not just for its ability to smell. When he finds her, he nudges her with his snout. Why does Rufus need to touch his owner?

Touch is more than when something is in contact with your skin. Touch also includes feeling texture, vibration, temperature, and pain. So, for example, when you hold an ice cube in your hand, you know it's touching your skin. But you also know it's smooth and cold. And if you hold it long enough, you'll feel icy pain.

Dogs experience touch much the same way you do. And that includes feeling pain, even though they don't always show it. Remember how dogs evolved from wolves? It's dangerous for wild animals to show their pain and look vulnerable because they could be picked on or attacked. That's why dogs still tend to keep their pain to themselves even though humans are here to help.

Dogs can sense temperature with their skin, just like you can. On top of that, their noses have a magic touch. That fur-free skin at the

WARM +

COOL −

end of a dog's snout can sense heat coming off another object—from as far away as 5 ft. (1.5 m)! That heat-seeking nose may have helped a dog's wolf ancestors find hidden prey. And it may explain why Rufus seeks his owner with his nose. Feeling her body heat lets him know she's really there.

PUPPY LOVE

A sense of smell is very important to a newborn puppy, but touch is also key. When separated from his mother, a puppy will use his heat-seeking nose to feel for her warmth. Then, when it's time to eat, he will use his paws to press against his mother's belly, a touch that starts the flow of her milk. In turn, his mother will nuzzle and groom him. And all that touching creates an emotional bond.

Wired with Whiskers

Dogs have another special tool for sensing touch that humans don't have—whiskers! Also called vibrissae (vai-BRI-see), these special hairs are found on a dog's chin, cheeks, muzzle, and even over her eyes to help her feel what's around her face. Think of whiskers as an early-warning system: the dog can avoid bumping into obstacles or getting too close to danger by paying attention to what her whiskers are telling her.

Whiskers are longer, stiffer, and thicker than the hair that makes up a dog's fur. And at the root of each whisker, there are plenty of cells called touch receptors that send messages to the brain when the whisker moves. In fact, each whisker signals its own area of the brain, so just like you know which fingertip is touching something, the dog knows which whisker is bent.

Whiskers are so sensitive they don't even have to touch an object for the dog to know something is there. Air currents around an object can move a whisker enough to alert the dog. Imagine how useful that is, especially in the dark. Plus, since dogs don't see details very well, whiskers help them sense the size and shape of objects near their mouths and eyes as well as help them know if they have enough room to fit through a small space. That's pretty smart for eyebrows and a beard!

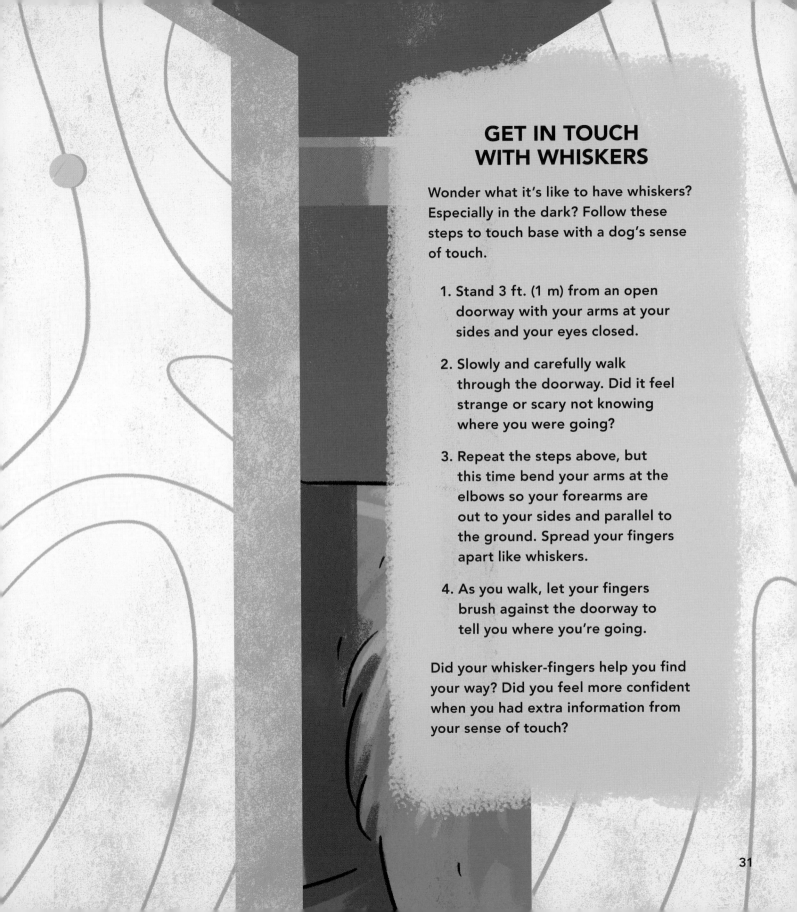

GET IN TOUCH WITH WHISKERS

Wonder what it's like to have whiskers? Especially in the dark? Follow these steps to touch base with a dog's sense of touch.

1. Stand 3 ft. (1 m) from an open doorway with your arms at your sides and your eyes closed.

2. Slowly and carefully walk through the doorway. Did it feel strange or scary not knowing where you were going?

3. Repeat the steps above, but this time bend your arms at the elbows so your forearms are out to your sides and parallel to the ground. Spread your fingers apart like whiskers.

4. As you walk, let your fingers brush against the doorway to tell you where you're going.

Did your whisker-fingers help you find your way? Did you feel more confident when you had extra information from your sense of touch?

Perceptive
Paws

Touch receptors aren't evenly spread over the human body. You have more in your fingertips than in your arm, for example. Similarly, dogs have loads more touch receptors in their noses and snouts compared to their backs. (When they stick their noses everywhere, they're getting more than just a good sniff.) Dogs also have a lot of touch receptors in their paws.

A dog's paws have many important jobs to do. They hold his weight and act like shock absorbers when he's running. They help regulate his temperature—sweat glands in his paws help keep him cool. And the special way blood moves through a dog's paws helps to keep the blood at a constant temperature, even when walking through cold snow.

A dog's paws also tell him about his environment, such as whether the ground is rough or smooth or cold or hot. That requires a lot of touch receptors, not only in the paw pads (the hairless patches of skin on the bottoms of a dog's feet), but between the pads and on top of the paws, too. This makes for some sensitive feet, so it's no wonder many dogs don't like to have their paws touched. And you thought *your* feet were ticklish!

CLAWS

A dog's claws have blood vessels and nerves running down the center. Claws are used for digging, gripping the ground while moving, and holding on to objects.

DIGITAL PADS

There are four of these smaller pads—one on each toe. They help the dog support his weight and feel the ground.

METACARPAL PAD

This large pad in the middle of each front paw also allows the dog to support his weight and sense the ground. On the back paws, this pad is called the metatarsal pad.

DEWCLAW

The dewclaw is almost like a doggy thumb, although dogs can't move and control them. Most dogs have dewclaws on their front legs, and some have them on their back legs, too.

THE KICK SPOT

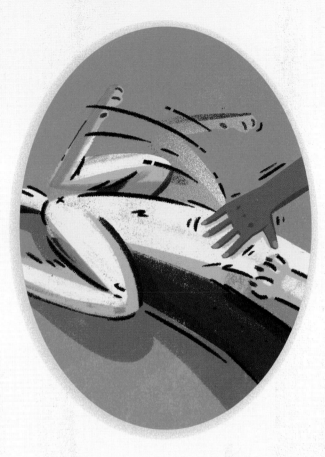

Have you ever noticed how some dogs kick their legs wildly when you scratch particular areas on their belly, back, or side? It's almost as if they can't help it. That's because they can't. This "scratch reflex" happens when receptors in that area of a dog's skin send a signal to her brain telling her leg to kick away the irritation. This probably evolved as a way of removing fleas or other pests. Not all dogs find rubs in the "kick spot" irritating, but just be sure that when a dog's scratch reflex kicks in, she's truly enjoying your attention.

Hearing Superheroes

An Airedale terrier named Lily seems to always know when her owner is coming home. It could be morning, noon, or night, but several minutes before the car pulls into the driveway, Lily barks at the front door. She is never barking up the wrong tree—is there something Lily hears that we can't?

Sounds are waves that travel through air, water, and even solid objects, such as the ground. These waves are created by a vibration (a quick movement back and forth). The faster the sound wave, the higher pitched the sound.

The speed of sound waves is measured in hertz (Hz). Some mouse squeaks measure well over 20,000 Hz and are so high-pitched, they're "silent" to the human ear. But an elephant's deep rumble, which is too low for human ears to hear, measures only around 12 Hz.

On average, humans can hear a range of sounds from as low as 20 Hz to as high as 20,000 Hz. Dogs, however, can hear sounds only as low as 65 Hz but at least as high as 45,000 Hz. That means they can hear things too high for human ears, including those mouse squeaks. From insects moving in the walls to the hum of the television, dogs are bathed in all sorts of high-pitched sounds you can't hear.

Why would a dog need to be such a hearing superhero? Like the development of so many of his senses, it might be thanks to his predatory past. Many rodents communicate with high squeaks, and the sound of prey scurrying through the brush makes high-pitched sounds, too. Being able to hear these noises would have made hunting much easier.

Not only can dogs hear higher sounds than we can, but they can probably hear quieter sounds, too. This might depend on the shape of a dog's ears, though. Scientists think upright ears like a German shepherd's collect sounds, while the floppy ears of a dog like a beagle block sounds. So then why would some breeds have floppy ears? Because humans bred them to look that way. And they do have their uses— remember the bloodhound? Those floppy ears help collect odors, which makes for better scent tracking.

But no matter their ear shape, the fact is that dogs hear a whole world of sounds we don't. Which likely explains how Lily knows when her owner is coming home—she knows the sound of her owner's car and can hear it from blocks away.

EAR TALK

Did you know dogs also "talk" with their ears? Although you need to look at a dog's whole body to truly know her mood, the position of a dog's ears can tell you a lot about how she's feeling.

A dog with her ears perked up might be feeling playful. A dog with her ears pinned back against her head is scared or stressed. Of course, dogs with floppy ears are harder to read than dogs with triangular, wolf-like ears.

35

All the **Better** to **Hear** You With

If dogs can hear sounds you can't, do their ears work differently than yours?
You might think so since dogs' ears look so different on the outside. Surprisingly, though, the inside of a dog's ear is built very much like a human's.

The outer part of a dog's ear is called the pinna (PIH-nuh) (or pinnae (PIH-nee) if you are referring to both ears). Dogs can move each of their pinna separately, which helps them determine where sounds are coming from. The pinna funnels sound waves into the ear canal, although an upright ear does this better than a floppy one.

Inside a dog's ear, the ear canal tends to be longer and wider than a human's. Once sound waves enter the ear canal, they continue on to the eardrum. The eardrum is a flap of skin stretched tightly across the ear canal. When a sound wave hits the eardrum, it vibrates—just like the surface of a drum that's been struck with a drumstick.

Behind the eardrum is the middle ear, which has three tiny bones called the incus (IN-kus), malleus (MAH-lee-us), and stapes (STAY-peez). These bones pick up the eardrum's vibrations and make them stronger as they carry them to the inner ear, which contains the cochlea (CO-klee-ah), a snail-shaped sack filled with fluid.

When vibrations travel from the middle ear to the cochlea, they make the fluid inside move in waves. These waves push tiny hairs that line the cochlea, which in turn send signals to the auditory nerve. The spiral of a dog's cochlea has more turns than ours, which might help the dog hear a wider range of sounds.

The auditory nerve carries the messages from the hairs in the cochlea to the brain. Then the brain figures out exactly what the dog has heard.

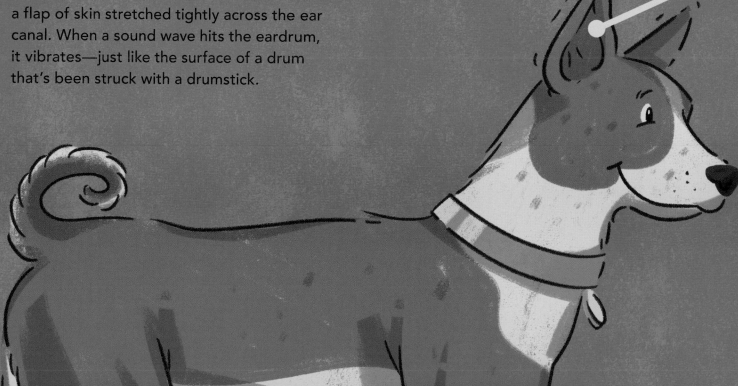

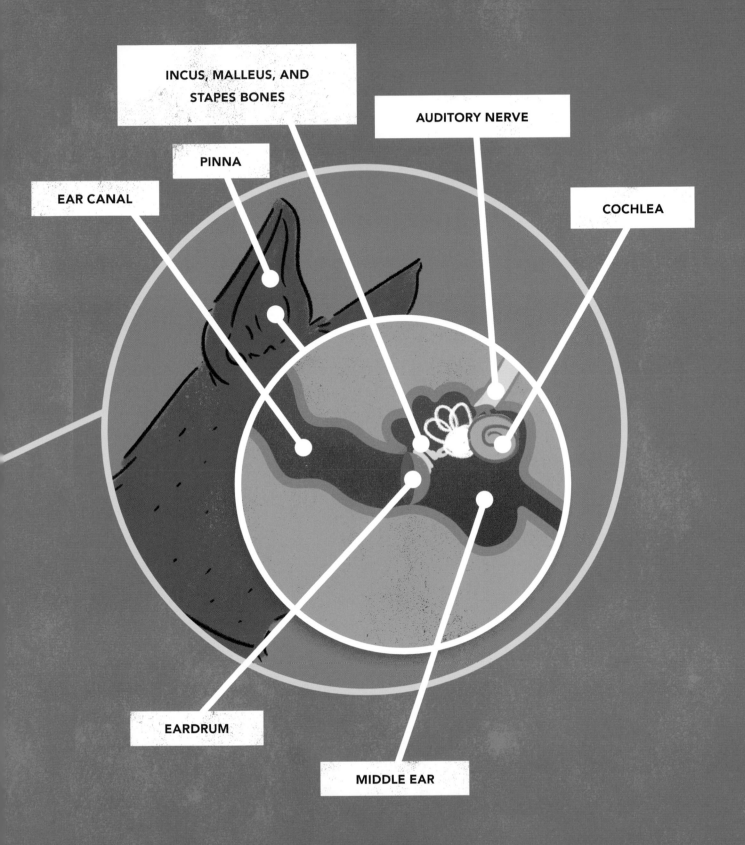

INCUS, MALLEUS, AND STAPES BONES

AUDITORY NERVE

PINNA

EAR CANAL

COCHLEA

EARDRUM

MIDDLE EAR

Here, Doggy, Doggy

When you hear a sound, you can usually tell where it's coming from. This is known as localization. Dogs localize sounds, too. It helps them find their human family and furry friends when they can't see them. And, of course, being able to localize the sound of prey is important when hunting. It also helps with avoiding danger: if a dog can locate a threatening sound, she can escape in the right direction.

To localize sounds, both dogs and people rely a lot on our brains. One way is by comparing the difference in time between when a sound wave hits one ear versus when it hits the other. For example, if it hits the right ear first, then the sound is coming from the right. The difference is teeny tiny—measured in microseconds—but that's enough.

Dog and human brains also compare the loudness and quality of the sound coming into each ear. When a sound comes from a particular side, it will be louder and clearer to the closer ear. Of course, where you might turn your whole head to try to locate that noise, dogs can just turn their ears.

RADAR EARS

Although some people can wiggle their ears, dogs have us beat when it comes to this trick. Dogs can move their ears in many different directions, making their pinnae like mini radar dishes that pinpoint sounds. You might think this makes dogs better than humans at localization. Surprisingly, though, studies have shown we localize sounds better than dogs! But that doesn't stop dogs from finding every squirrel in the yard.

HEAR, THERE, AND EVERYWHERE

What if you had pinnae like a dog's? Would it make a difference to how well you hear? Try giving yourself dog ears.

1. Turn on some music so you can just barely hear it.

2. Cup each hand in the shape of a C. Then place your hands around the backs of your ears so they funnel sound like a German shepherd's ears. Can you hear the music better now?

3. Move your cupped hands around your ears. Does the position of your hands change how well you can hear? How about how well you can locate the source of the music?

4. Now hold your hands flat over your ears like the floppy ears of a beagle. Is the music more difficult to hear? Is it harder to locate the source of the music this way, even if you move your head around?

Did adding German shepherd ears help your hearing? How did beagle ears sound? Now you know how ear shape might affect how different dogs hear.

Do Dogs Have a Sixth Sense?

Sometimes it seems like dogs have extra senses we don't. They might predict somebody's arrival, just like Lily the Airedale terrier. Or magically find hidden objects, like Remi the Labrador retriever. But as we've learned, these are actually examples of how dogs' senses are more powerful than yours.

There are many stories about lost dogs who return home after walking incredibly long distances through areas they have never been before. Take Bobbie the Wonder Dog. After getting lost while on a family trip to Indiana in 1923, Bobbie found his way home to Oregon six months later. That's a trip of over 2,500 mi. (4,020 km)!

Or what about World War I courier dogs like Satan, who carried messages between headquarters and the faraway battlefield? In 1916, he saved a group of French soldiers who, trapped by the enemy, had no way to communicate with their commanding officers. Satan arrived through a spray of gunfire to bring a message to the soldiers saying backup was coming the next day. Wearing a gas mask and carrying two homing pigeons in cages strapped to his shoulders, Satan had traveled by himself all the way from headquarters.

How did Bobbie and Satan find their way? It's almost like dogs have a built-in compass to help them navigate. The fact is—they do. Our planet is like a giant magnet, and the north and south poles are its two magnetic ends. Many animals, such as sea turtles and migrating birds, can sense the pull of the two poles, just like the magnetic needles of a compass can. Scientists think dogs also share this ability, known as magnetoreception (mag-NEE-toe-ree-SEP-shun).

Using this "sixth sense," dogs can find specific locations without relying solely on their sense of smell or vision. And in fact, dogs are so aware of the poles, they often poop lined up in a north-south position as well. While nobody knows why dogs use their internal compass for pooping, it makes sense that they possess magnetoreception. It would help them return home after hunting or tracking. Plus, dogs' wolf ancestors would have had to navigate huge territories—some over 1,000 sq. mi. (2,500 sq. km).

And before you get too disappointed about lacking this "sixth sense," some scientists have thrown you a bone—new research hints that humans might have magnetoreception, too.

CAN DOGS PREDICT EARTHQUAKES?

There are many tales of dogs getting restless
before an earthquake. Is this another
sense? Or another example of their higher
sensitivity? In other words, perhaps it's that
dogs can hear the high-pitched sounds of
rocks rubbing together or smell the release
of gases from deep in the Earth that humans
can't. Or it could be that they feel vibrations
or sense shifts in the Earth's magnetic field.
It's tempting to think dogs have another sense
that can be our earthquake early-warning
system, but scientists have yet to prove how
they do it or even if they can.

Through a
Dog's Senses

Now that you have a better understanding of the unique ways dogs see, smell, taste, touch, and hear, have you figured out the key to some of their grosser behaviors?

What about when dogs roll in poop? Why would an animal with such a strong sense of smell want to stink so badly? Chances are it's to advertise the smell to others, a kind of "hey, look at the cool thing I found" behavior. Because, as you know, what smells gross to a human is not always what smells gross to a dog. And what smells good to a human is not always what smells good to a dog. In other words, dogs would much rather wear poop perfume than stink like flowery dog shampoo.

Then there's drinking out of the toilet bowl. When you look at it from a dog's sensory point of view, it's not disgusting at all. A dog's tongue is tuned in to the taste of water.

And clean toilet water is cooler and fresher than what has been sitting in the water dish since yesterday.

So many of the things we find odd about dogs make sense if you imagine you have their senses. This knowledge also helps us meet dogs' needs. If you're lucky enough to live with a dog, don't treat her like a furry human. Let her be a dog. That might mean letting her drink from the toilet bowl (as long as it's been flushed and there are no cleaning products in the water) or letting her roll in stinky stuff (as long as you're willing to give her a bath). Or it might be as simple as allowing her to sniff every fire hydrant on your daily walks. If you remember how her senses work and allow her to use them fully, you'll be sure to have a happy pup.

SAYING HELLO IN DOG LANGUAGE

It's always a good idea to greet dogs in their language. No, this doesn't mean sniffing butts! But it does mean respecting doggy culture and saying hello appropriately. Here are some tips:

- Dogs can find eye contact threatening, so never stare into the eyes of a dog you don't know.
- Always let them smell you before you reach out to pet them.
- Don't hug a dog no matter how adorable he is. Some dogs will put up with it, but most hate hugs and would much rather play a game or get a treat.

Senses Showdown

Dogs have noses and whiskers that seem to give them *sense*-sational superpowers, and the world sounds completely different to them than it does to us. But think of their poor sense of taste and blurry eyesight. Are you surprised that some of your senses are better than theirs? *Fur* the fun of it, let's see how your senses stack up against theirs.

VISION

In daylight, you can see more clearly than a dog can. And you see in a brighter rainbow of colors. But dogs can see with far less light than you can. And they are great at seeing movement.

SMELL

Dogs experience life through their sense of smell. Their noses give them abilities we can only imagine having, like detecting diseases or searching for explosives.

TASTE

You have far more taste receptors than dogs do. Plus, you're more sensitive to the taste of salt. However, unlike you, dogs can taste water.

HEARING

Dogs can move their ears like radar dishes, but you can still pinpoint the source of a sound better. Then again, although you can hear lower sounds than dogs, dogs can hear sounds that are far higher.

TOUCH

You have a sensitive sense of touch. But dogs have heat-seeking noses and snouts full of whiskers that help them see without their eyes.

PERFECT AS WE ARE

Although we can have fun rating our senses, the truth is it doesn't matter. Dogs are perfectly suited to being dogs. And you are perfectly suited to being a human. It's not about how dogs compare to us, but how we each use our senses to survive and thrive. Dogs may have the senses of a predator, but on their journey from wolves to family pets, they became our best friends.

—Glossary—

Carnivore: an animal that gets most of its food by eating other animals, also known as a meat-eater

Disturbance odor: the smell left behind when somebody walks across the ground and crushes plants and insects

Domesticated animal: an animal that has been bred over generations to live as a pet or serve humans in some way

Evolution: how the characteristics of animals and other living organisms change gradually over many generations

Hertz (Hz): a measurement of the frequency of a sound. Higher-pitched sounds have a higher number of hertz

Localization: the ability to recognize or locate where a sound is coming from

Magnetoreception: the ability to sense the Earth's magnetic field

Pack: a group of animals who live and hunt together

Pheromones: special chemicals animals give off to communicate with each other

Predator: an animal that hunts and kills other animals for food

Proprioception: the ability to sense the location and movement of one's body

Receptor: a special cell that senses information from its environment

Scavenger: an animal that gets most of its food from dead animals, rotting plants, or garbage

Scent particles: invisible odor molecules

Tame animal: a wild animal that has become used to people

Track: to recognize and follow the scent or other evidence left behind by an animal or human

Umami: the taste sensation of savory or meaty

Vibrissae: thick hairs, also known as whiskers, that are used for sensing nearby objects

Visual acuity: how clear objects appear when seen from a distance

FETCHING FURTHER FACTS

Hirsch, Andy. *Science Comics: Dogs: From Predator to Protector*. New York: First Second, 2017.

Horowitz, Alexandra. *Inside of a Dog: What Dogs See, Smell, and Know*. Young Readers Edition. New York: Simon & Schuster Books for Young Readers, 2016.

Horowitz, Alexandra. *Our Dogs, Ourselves: How We Live with Dogs*. Young Readers Edition. New York: Simon & Schuster Books for Young Readers, 2020.

Moore, Arden. *A Kid's Guide to Dogs: How to Train, Care for, and Play and Communicate with Your Amazing Pet!* North Adams, MA: Storey Publishing, 2020.

Wadsworth, Ginger. *Poop Detectives: Working Dogs in the Field*. Watertown, MA: Charlesbridge, 2016.

Warren, Cat. *What the Dog Knows: Scent, Science, and the Amazing Ways Dogs Perceive the World*. Young Readers Edition. New York: Simon & Schuster Books for Young Readers, 2019.

Wheeler-Toppen, Jodi. *Dog Science Unleashed: Fun Activities to Do with Your Canine Companion*. Washington, DC: National Geographic Kids, 2018.

INDEX